DEDICATION

In loving memory of my Mother Ann Irene Terrell

&

To my son's Kenny and Cameron who hold my infinite love.

Barbara Allen

Remembering Great Grandma – Sojourner Truth
By Barbara Allen

Text & Illustrations copyright © 2021 by Barbara Allen

Library of Congress
Published by AK Classics

PAPERBACK
ISBN-13: 978-1-7357964-7-5
ISBN-10: 1-7357964-7-6

Illustrations by Cristal Baldwin (FlyingFrogStudio.net)
Graphic Design by Marcia Noisette (NoisetteInk.com)

REFERENCE

Battle Creek Enquirer - April 30, 1999

100 Women Encyclopedia Sojourner Truth
https://www.britannica.com/explore/100women/profiles/sojourner-truth

The Slave Narratives of Sojourner Truth, [Great Grandma's Religious Experience], 1850)
http://digital.library.upenn.edu/women/truth/1850/1850.html#19

AK Classics
P.O. Box 77203
Charlotte, NC 28271
www.akclassicstories.com

★REMEMBERING★
GREAT GRANDMA
SOJOURNER TRUTH

Written by
ARBARA ALLEN

Illustrated by
RISTAL BALDWIN

Remembering Great Grandma
Sojourner Truth

INTRODUCTION

Welcome children! This is a dynamic picture book of the most incredible abolitionist and women's rights leader of all time. You may have heard of her from history classes and the documentaries. Still, I know her through family history and stories handed down through generations of my family. You see, I am Sojourner Truth's great-granddaughter. That is why I refer to her in this book as Great Grandma.

Great Grandma was born into slavery. Slavery is a challenging and brutalizing life. She was sold several times by the age of 13. Throughout Grandma's time as a slave, she was beaten and treated inhumanely. But her worst pain and suffering came when she was forced to watch her parents die from mistreatment and neglect.

By the grace of God, she was able to escape the brutality of slavery by the time she was a young woman. Although she was now free, she did not take her freedom for granted. Great Grandma traveled throughout the country, speaking out against slavery, and speaking up for women's rights. When slavery ended, she started working for better conditions for the freed slaves. She continued her work on behalf of women's rights.

Great Grandma could not read or write, but her words were powerful and helped people even to this day understand slavery's brutality. All people deserve equal and fair treatment.

"Remembering Great Grandma – Sojourner Truth" is the exciting children's story of a woman who believed in God and herself. She was determined to survive her adversities and live on to speak the truth.

"Mommy, mommy," I would say to my mother when I was a child, "Tell me about my Great, Great, Great, Great Grandma." "Ok, sweetie," my ever-loving and patient mother would say to me. She would smile and tuck me into bed, then say in a soft, calming voice, "Now snuggle in." As my mother said to me, I now say to you, "Snuggle in" and take this journey into the life and times of a most remarkable woman. My Great Grandma.

My Great Grandma was a
remarkable person. Her name is
Sojourner Truth.

Great Grandma was born into slavery as Isabella Baumfree in New York around 1797.

Her parents were James and Elizabeth Baumfree – (Mau Mau Bet). They were among many Africans captured from the Gold Coast, currently called Ghana, and brought over to America as slaves.

Great Grandma had a large family of ten brothers and sisters.

James and Elizabeth loved their children very much. When it was quiet, they would tell their children about their life in Ghana and the God they worshiped back home. Does anyone tell you stories about the time long ago?

Great Grandma's parents would tell her that God loved everyone equally, and He would protect her always.

Great Grandma loved these stories, and when it was nighttime, she would sneak out and find a quiet place and sing quietly to the full moon sky. She would sing, "Come by here, my Lord, come by here; oh Lord, come by here."

Great Grandma always felt that she had more purpose in life than working in the fields and being a slave. But she was a good girl, and she obeyed her parents. Do you obey your parents?

As Great Grandma grew older, her siblings were sold one by one to other slave owners. She became lonely and scared that she would be next.

When Great Grandma was nine years old, her worst fear happened. She was taken away from her parents and put on the auction block to be sold with a flock of sheep to an English man named John Neely.

Have you ever thought about what it would be like to be taken away from your parents? Perhaps now is an excellent time to give your parents a hug and let them know how much you love them.

Great Grandma was very afraid. She had never been away from her parents, and she only spoke Dutch, so she could not understand what anyone was saying.

On the ride to Mr. Neely's home, she began to sing silently, "Come by here, my Lord, come by here. Oh Lord, come by here," until she fell asleep.

Since Great Grandma spoke only Dutch and did not understand English, she would get into trouble making mistakes. Mrs. Neely would slap her often.

One day Mr. Neely took her out to the barn and beat Great Grandma so severely that she passed out on the ground.

When she regained consciousness, she was covered in sweat, blood, and tears. She heard a voice say, "I am here, my child, I am here." This gave Great Grandma the strength to make it through another day.

Not long after that terrible beating, Great Grandma's father came to visit. She was so happy when she saw him, "Papa Papa," she cried.

Great Grandma's father was concerned about her. She looked so tired and frail while James himself appeared old and worn. They both put their worries aside and embraced each other for hours.

Great Grandma asked her father how is Mau Mau Bet. Her father said, "Doing well." But that was not true. Mau Mau Bet was quite ill and fragile.

Great Grandma and her father sat underneath an old oak tree and talked and talked. She asked her father to tell her about God in Ghana. He told her the same story he always had. "God loves everyone equally and is still beside you. Trust in His power, and He will see you through." That gave Great Grandma comfort.

Shortly after that, a man named Martin Schryver, a friend of James, purchased Great Grandma and moved her to his property.

For the next two years, Great Grandma lived with the Schryvers. She grew tall and strong. She looked very much like her father.

Great Grandma worked hard. Most days, she had to unload the fishing boats, plant and hoe corn in the field, and work in the Schryver's tavern.

While Great Grandma was living at the Schryvers, she found out both of her parents had died. First Mau-Mau Bet and then Papa James. Great Grandma was sad, but happy they were finally resting with the Lord.

One day, a man came into the Schryver's tavern, and upon seeing Great Grandma, wanted to buy her for three times what Mr. Schryver had paid for her. His name was John Dumont. Though he liked Great Grandma. Mr. Schryver could not resist such an attractive offer. So he sold Great Grandma for $300, which was a lot of money in those days.

Great Grandma labored hard on the Dumont farm. Mr. Dumont always boasted that Great Grandma worked harder than any male slave. Great Grandma was around thirteen and nearly six feet tall. Some observers said that despite Great Grandma being a slave, she looked and carried herself like an African queen. Can you name an African queen?

Around 1817 Mr. Dumont decided Great Grandma, now around 20 years of age, needed a husband. He picked one of his field slaves named Thomas. How would you feel if someone picked your husband or wife for you? Of course, it is necessary to point out that Mr. Dumont's concern was not for Great Grandma. His interest was in Great Grandma having children which he could sell, and in so doing, improve his profits.

One year later, Great Grandma and Thomas had a daughter named Diana. Within the next ten years, they had four more children: Elizabeth-named after Great Grandma's mother, Hannah, Peter, and Sophia.

In 1817, a new law was passed in New York State. Slaves born before July 4, 1799 had to be freed by July 4, 1827, which meant Great Grandma and her husband would be released in about ten years.

Better Yet! Dumont promised that he would free Great Grandma and Thomas earlier if Great Grandma worked extra hard in the coming years.

Great Grandma began to work extra hard. She worked in the fields planting crops and in the house washing, cooking, cleaning, and making clothes.

One day while Great Grandma was in the field, she cut her hand on a sharp tool. She was determined to get free, so she wrapped her hand and continued to work hard.

When it became time for Mr. Dumont to free Great Grandma and James, he changed his mind. He did not feel that Great Grandma had worked hard enough with an injured hand.

Great Grandma could not wait any longer. She woke up early one morning, packed up a pillowcase, picked up her youngest daughter Sophia, and walked away from slavery. She left her other children with James.

Great Grandma met many interesting people along the way who were nice to her and Sophia and gave them refuge in their home.

Great Grandma began to preach the word of the Lord and one day she heard the Lord say, "Journey throughout the land and preach the truth." Great Grandma heeded the call, changed her name to "Sojourner Truth", and made plans to start her journey.

Sojourner spent years preaching at women's rights conferences and outdoor church meetings.
She met many influential people like William Lloyd Garrison, Frederick Douglass, Susan B. Anthony, and even President Lincoln. Sojourner was true to her name and faithful to her God.

After many years, your great, great, great, great Grandma found her way to Battle Creek, Michigan with her daughter Sophia to live out the rest of her life.

Wow, Mommy, that was a great story. Tell me again how she is my Great Grandma?

Well, Barbara, Sojourner's daughter Sophia married Thomas Schuyler. They had a daughter named Fannie, and she married Frank Liechty, who later changed the family name to McLiechey. He had a son Thomas McLiechey which was my grandfather. His daughter Juanita gave birth to me, and I gave birth to a special little girl who is you…

Then my mother said, "I want you to always remember you are connected to an incredibly special person. Your Great Grandma risked her life leaving that morning with her daughter Sophia so that you would one day have a life of freedom and opportunity."

"Shine your light on this world and always honor her legacy." She then kissed me on the cheek as she was leaving the room. I began to quietly sing "Kumbaya my Lord, Kumbaya, Oh Lord Kumbaya" until I fell asleep.

VISION
Barbara M. Allen

I had a vision of a woman who was larger than life.
She was in a field picking cotton, trying to forget her pain and strife.
She was singing, "Glory to God in the Highest.
Glory to the Almighty King."
He saved me, watched over me, and soon he will set me free.
In my vision, this woman worked her fingers to the bone.
Waiting on the Lord to reveal her new home
She was set free from bondage.
And walked away a Queen.
She said, "I will change my name and help set other captives free."
She journeyed throughout the land.
Speaking about truth and honor
Not once ever worrying about how she would make a dollar.
For her mission had been planned before the beginning of time.
To preach about freedom for your children and mine.
This woman was my Great-Grandma.
And she never ever knew
That the legacy she left behind
Would someday see me through.
I give glory to **Sojourner**
I give honor to God
For had he not created her
We would not be as far.

 **AUTHOR BIO**

BARBARA M. ALLEN is a sixth-generation granddaughter of Sojourner Truth. When Sojourner Truth walked away to freedom in 1826, she took her daughter Sophia with her. Sophia married Thomas Schuyler and they had a daughter named Fannie, who married Frank McLiechey. Their son Thomas was Barbara Allen's great grandfather. His daughter Juanita gave birth to Allen's Mother, Ann Irene Terrell.

Barbara always remembers the stories that her mother would tell her about Sojourner Truth. After many years of researching and examining documents chronicling Great Grandma's accomplishments and achievements, Barbara began to realize that Great Grandma was more impressive than her mother could put into words. Barbara decided not only to put into words but also illustrate the fantastic story that she heard as a child.

Barbara's accomplishments include an MBA, a Post-graduate degree in Human Resources, and she is an avid student of theology.

Barbara has written this book to educate young children about an amazing woman whose belief and courage saw her through the storm.

Contact Barbara Allen:
Website: sixth-generation.com
Email: barbara@sixth-generation.com